NATIVE AMERICAN MYTHS

By Anita Dalal

Gareth Stevens
Publishing

Please visit our Web site www.garethstevens.com. For a free color catalog of all our high-quality books, call toll free 1-800-542-2595 or fax 1-877-542-2596.

Library of Congress Cataloging-in-Publication Data
Dalal, Anita.
    Native American myths / [retold by] Anita Dalal.
        p. cm. -- (Myths from around the world)
    Includes index.
    ISBN 978-1-4339-3530-5 (library binding) -- ISBN 978-1-4339-3531-2 (pbk.)
    ISBN 978-1-4339-3532-9 (6-pack)
    1. Indian mythology--North America--Juvenile literature.
    2. Indians of North America--Religion--Juvenile literature. I. Title.
E98.R3D1353 2010
299.7--dc22   2009038713

Published in 2010 by
Gareth Stevens Publishing
111 East 14th Street, Suite 349
New York, NY 10003

© 2010 The Brown Reference Group Ltd.

For Gareth Stevens Publishing:
Art Direction: Haley Harasymiw
Editorial Direction: Kerri O'Donnell

For The Brown Reference Group Ltd:
Editorial Director: Lindsey Lowe
Managing Editor: Tim Cooke
Editor: Henry Russell
Children's Publisher: Anne O'Daly
Picture Manager: Sophie Mortimer
Design Manager: David Poole
Designers: Tim Mayer and John Walker
Production Director: Alastair Gourlay

Picture Credits:
Front Cover: Jupiter Images: Stockxpert b, br; Shutterstock: Jstock t

Corbis: Jonathan Blair 11; Gene Blevins 41b; Burstein Collection 13t; The Mariners Museum 25; iStock: Bob Ainsworth 13b; Grafissimo 37; Rod Kay 3; Manook 21t, MPI/Getty Images 8, Paco Romero 9; Cliff Walken 21b; Jupiter Images: Photos.com 16, 45; Stockxpert 27, 32, 39, 43; Library of Congress: 5, 12, 17b, 29, 36, 41t; Shutterstock: 31; Jill Battaglia 40; Jan Bruder 23; Dennis Donohue 15; Lindsay Douglas 7; Jstock 19; Yuriy Kulyk 24; Schalke Fotografie 44; SebStock 28; John S. Sfondilias 28; B.G. Smith 20

Publisher's note to educators and parents: Our editors have carefully reviewed the Web sites that appear on p. 47 to ensure that they are suitable for students. Many Web sites change frequently, however, and we cannot guarantee that a site's future contents will continue to meet our high standards of quality and educational value. Be advised that students should be closely supervised whenever they access the Internet.

Manufactured in the United States of America
1 2 3 4 5 6 7 8 9 12 11 10

CPSIA compliance information: Batch #BRW0102GS: For further information contact Gareth Stevens, New York, New York at 1-800-542-2595.

3 9082 11209 1916

Contents

Introduction

Myths are mirrors of humanity. They reflect the soul of a culture and try to give profound answers in a seemingly mysterious world. They give the people an understanding of their place in the world and the universe.

Found in all civilizations, myths sometimes combine fact and fiction and at other times are complete fantasy.

Every culture has its own myths. Yet, globally, there are common themes, even across civilizations that had no contact with each other. The most common myths deal with the creation of the world or of a particular site, like a mountain or a lake. Other myths deal with the origin of humans or describe the heroes and gods who either made the world inhabitable or who provided humans with something essential, such as the ancient Greek Titan Prometheus, who gave fire, and the Native American Wunzh, who was given divine instructions on cultivating corn. There are also myths about the end of the world, death, and the afterlife.

The origin of evil and death are also common themes. Examples of such myths are the Biblical Eve eating the forbidden fruit and the ancient Greek story of Pandora opening the sealed box.

Additionally, there are flood myths, myths about the sun and the moon, and myths of peaceful places of reward, such as heaven or Elysium, and of places of punishment, such as hell or Tartarus. Myths also teach human values, such as courage and honesty.

This book deals with some of the Native Americans' most important myths. A glossary at the end of the book identifies the major mythological and historical characters and explains cultural terms.

Native American Mythology

When Christopher Columbus landed on the Caribbean island of San Salvador in 1492, North America was populated by several million people. Most of these peoples lived in small communities, many of which were linked by a similar or a common language. Each tribe had myths that related to its own way of life and included explanations of the existence of water, corn, fish, and buffalo.

This painting by George Catlin from about 1850 shows a Crow tepee decorated with scenes of war and buffalo hunting. Native Americans had many myths about buffalo, which were very important to their lives.

Native Americans believed that the spirit world originated and controlled all nature. As in many cultures around the world, Native American myths were reflected in rituals. Often celebrated using a combination of face- and body-painting, chanting and singing, dancing, and playing music, their rituals portrayed scenes from myths.

Shamans, or medicine men, were responsible for maintaining a good relationship between the tribe and the spirit world. Shamans commanded enormous influence in the community. They were highly perceptive individuals who had to go through a long period of training before they could be expected to fully understand and communicate with the supernatural.

The Dueling Brothers

The Iroquois, who originated this myth, were one of the largest tribes in the vast Eastern Woodlands region, ranging from the Great Lakes and the Mississippi River to the Atlantic seaboard.

At the beginning of time, high in the sky, lived the Great Chief, his wife, and the celestial people. There was a thin, hard crust at the bottom of their sky village and no one knew what lay beneath it. In the center of the sky village grew a huge tree.

One day, the Great Chief's wife told her husband that she was pregnant. Angry at this news, the Great Chief pulled up the tree and pushed his wife into the hole.

The hole led through the clouds. As the Chief's wife was falling, two ducks living on the water-covered world below caught her on their outstretched wings and took her to their chief, the Great Turtle.

The Great Turtle knew that dirt from the roots of the celestial tree must have fallen down with the woman. He commanded all the animals to search for it, and it was eventually found by the little toad.

The toad spread the dirt onto the Great Turtle's shell. The dirt grew magically into an island for the Great Chief's wife.

Twins of Good and Evil

Months later, the Great Chief's wife gave birth to a daughter. For many years they lived happily until one day the daughter was made pregnant by the wind. She gave birth to twins. The older twin was good, but the younger twin was evil and killed his mother as she gave birth to him.

The boys were raised by the Great Chief's wife. The older boy, Tsentsa, planted fruit trees and pretty bushes. The younger boy, Taweskare, tried to undo all his brother's good works. He made the fruit small and covered the bushes in thorns. When Tsentsa made fish smooth, Taweskare covered them in sharp scales. Taweskare made the snakes poisonous and the wintertime cold.

Tsentsa defeated his evil brother, and Taweskare was forced to go west. There his anger created many volcanoes that still belch smoke and cause the earth to tremble. Tsentsa stayed in the east and became the father of the Iroquois.

Native Americans believed that the steam from hydrothermal springs, such as these in Lassen Volcanic Park, California, was produced by Taweskare.

Adapting to Survive

North America is a land and climate of extremes, and each tribe faced its own set of struggles with nature to survive. The obstacles ranged from ice to drought, from bears to rattlesnakes.

Native America can be divided into 10 culture areas, each with its own unique environment— the Arctic, the Subarctic, the Northwest Coast, California, the Basin, the Plateau, the Southwest, the Great Plains, the Southeast, and the Eastern Woodlands.

Lessons of History

Survival techniques were passed down to Native Americans from ancient peoples such as the Adena and Mississippians, who built large cities with ceremonial mounds in the South, and the Anasazi and Hohokam, who farmed in the dry Southwest. These peoples thrived hundreds of years before tribes such as the Iroquois.

The Iroquois were actually a union of six tribes, also known as the Iroquois Confederacy, who lived in the vast Eastern Woodlands. These tribes were the

This painting by George Catlin (1796–1872) shows Native Americans of the Plains hunting a bear.

These are some of the adobe homes built by Pueblo Native Americans of the Southwest United States.

Mohawk, the Oneida, the Onondaga, the Cayuga, the Seneca, and the Tuscarora. Their union, or league, was formed between 1570 and 1600, long before European settlers came.

These tribes spoke similar languages and shared a common way of life. They lived in small enclosed villages made up of longhouses and farmed and hunted in the same way. The Iroquois, like most other major Eastern Woodlands tribes, hunted deer and moose, fished in rivers and lakes, and planted crops that included corn, beans, and squashes.

The Plains tribes, like the Sioux, had no fixed home but moved across the wide-open, flat spaces in pursuit of buffalo.

The tribes of the Southwest region—the Pueblo, the Hopi, and the Navajo—were primarily farmers. They developed irrigation systems that helped them grow crops such as corn, beans, and squashes. They lived in pueblos—permanent structures made of adobe, sometimes embedded in giant rockfaces.

In the Arctic, peoples such as the Inuit hunted for food in a landscape that was frozen for much of the year. The Inuit arrived in North America nearly 30,000 years after the first group of nomads crossed the Bering Strait into Alaska around 33,000 B.C. The Inuit relied on fishing and hunting marine mammals such as whales, seals, and walruses.

The Hopi in the Desert

The Hopi created this myth to try to explain the origin and diversity of tribes and languages in the Southwest. This myth is similar to certain myths told by other tribes of the region.

A very long time ago, the ancient people, who were the forefathers of all the tribes, lived underground, in a perfect paradise where everyone was happy. After a while, the ancient people began to take their perfect life for granted. They became lazy and greedy, demanding things that they did not need.

As punishment for the ancient people's ingratitude, the spirits of the underworld made the water in all the ponds, lakes, and rivers rise. Soon all the houses and villages were flooded. Only Spider Woman and Mockingbird felt sorry for the ancient people. Together they decided to help them escape.

Spider Woman showed the ancient people to a giant reed that led to two types of large pine tree. The tops of the trees were joined to a huge sunflower that rose to a tunnel high above the rising water. Mockingbird sat at the entrance of the tunnel, assigning a tribe and a language to each person as they entered.

To one person he sang, "You will belong to the Hopi and speak their language," to another, "You are now an Apache and will speak their tongue," or "You will be one of the Navajo and talk the way they talk."

There were so many people that Mockingbird sang for several long days. Eventually he grew too tired to sing, leaving many people trapped in the underworld without a tribe or a language.

Into the Light

All those who had been given a tribe and a language climbed through the tunnel to a desert on the earth's surface.

In those days, the earth was still covered in darkness, so the ancient people decided to set off in search of sunlight. They agreed that each tribe should travel in different directions. The so-called White People, who were a separate group of Hopi, went east, while the other tribes started off on foot in all directions. Only the remaining Hopi and

A spectacular meteor shower glows above a meteorite crater in Arizona.

the other Pueblo peoples stayed in the desert where they had surfaced.

The tribes agreed that the first group to find the sun would signal to all the other tribes by sending shooting stars across the sky. When they saw this sign, the other tribes would stop wherever they were and make that place their home.

The White People did not want to travel on foot. Their women rubbed flakes of skin from their bodies and molded them into horses. They rode quickly to the east, where the sun rises, and so became the first tribe to see it.

As promised, the White People sent a shower of stars racing across the sky, and when the other tribes saw the shooting stars they stopped traveling and settled. This is why the Hopi and Pueblo peoples, who had not moved, live in the desert.

The Evolution of Languages

When Christopher Columbus claimed the so-called New World for Spain in 1492, there were millions of people in North America speaking hundreds of languages and dialects.

Although the Hopi myth (see page 10) does not specify how many languages Mockingbird assigned to the different Native American peoples, anthropologists believe that before the arrival of European settlers North America (north of Mexico) was home to about 240 different tribes or peoples, with as many as 500 distinct languages.

The 500 different languages can then be divided further into at least 2,000 separate dialects. With so many different tongues among a population of only around 10 million, communication was often difficult between neighboring tribes and even within a single tribe. This lack of understanding remained until the tribes began trading with each other.

European culture took over many pre-Columbian traditions as Native Americans were educated in schools like this one in Carlisle, Pennsylvania.

SEQUOYA

In the early nineteenth century, Sequoya, a Cherokee trader and scholar, created the first Native American alphabet. His notation turned Cherokee, which was a Southeastern branch of Iroquoian, from a purely spoken language into one that could be written and read. Sequoya assigned a phonetic system that included a set of symbols that represented the 86 sounds making up the language. He completed his alphabet in 1821, and seven years later the first Native American newspaper, *The Cherokee Phoenix*, was published.

Spreading Languages

Over hundreds of years, as tribes moved around North America, their languages went with them. It was possible for two tribes who spoke a related language to end up thousands of miles away from each other. For example, the Navajo and the Apache tribes of the Southwest speak Athapascan languages, which are related to those of the peoples of the Subarctic. The other major tribal language groups include Algonquian, Caddoan, Iroquoian, Muskogean, and Siouan.

Despite so many different languages and dialects, by the early twentieth century, the dominance of white settlers had forced most North American Indian languages into virtual extinction. Some tribal languages are still vibrant, however. For example, there are over 100,000 tribespeople on reservations who speak Navajo.

Although traditional tepees such as this still exist, many Native Americans today live in European-style homes.

Old Man Coyote Creates Nature

The Crow tribe of Native Americans, who lived in modern-day Wyoming and Montana, believed that before the great animal spirits made the world, water covered everything. Many tribes had similar beliefs.

A long time ago, the earth was completely covered with water. Old Man Coyote, who lived on his own, was bored and wanted someone to talk to. One day he met two ducks.

"Is there nothing here but water?" he asked them. The ducks didn't know, but one of them dove down deep to find out.

When the duck resurfaced, he was carrying a little root and some mud. Old Man Coyote blew on the mud, and it began to grow and spread everywhere. He then took the root and planted it in the ground. Soon plants and trees grew, full of flowers and food to eat. Then he made rivers, ponds, and springs.

Old Man Coyote used the mud to make people, then more ducks, and finally buffalo, deer, elk, antelope, and bears. Now there were lots of people and animals, but they were bored because they had nothing to do.

Why Bears Hibernate

To liven up things, Old Man Coyote molded a bird who danced at dawn and a drum to make music. Soon all the animals were dancing too—all except the bears, who wanted a dance of their own. Old Man Coyote punished them, saying, "You will sleep half the year and live in a den all alone and eat rotten food." From that time on, that is how bears have lived.

Old Man Coyote then made a fire with lightning, and the people were pleased because they could cook and keep warm. Realizing that the people needed to kill animals for food, he made weapons. He also separated the people into tribes that spoke different languages.

A member of the dog family, the coyote plays a major role in many Native American myths and legends.

Native American Ceremonies

Life-changing events, such as birth, death, and war, were ritually celebrated by Native Americans, as were issues of survival, such as the harvest and the hunt.

The tribes of Native America depended heavily on wildlife, and that is why animals feature in so many of their myths.

Native Americans paid tribute to nature and the spirits, which they believed controlled all aspects of life, in elaborate rituals involving the local community and sometimes the whole tribe. The rituals were held to influence and celebrate important changes in people's lives, such as birth, marriage, and death, and the concerns of the community, such as a good harvest, a successful hunt, and victory in battle.

During public ceremonies, the performers would paint their faces or bodies and spend hours and sometimes days dancing, singing, and chanting to music played on drums, rattles, and flutes.

This painting depicts a ceremonial dance of the Sioux, a Native American people of the Dakotas, Iowa, Minnesota, and parts of Canada.

A Native American man wears a buffalo head to appease the spirits of the herd.

Funeral Rites

Other ceremonies involved rituals surrounding death. Most tribes believed that the dead could affect the world of the living, and so Native American funerals were meant to make sure that the spirits of the dead were kept happy. In the Eastern Woodlands, the Iroquois held an annual celebration known as the Feast of the Dead. Although it was specifically for those who had died during the previous year, the spirits of all dead people were invited so that they would know that they were still remembered and respected.

The snowshoe dance was part of a Subarctic Native American ritual to thank the spirits for the start of winter.

The Sun Dance

Dance held a deep religious significance for Native Americans. The Sun Dance ceremony, practiced by many Plains tribes, was held annually in early summer. During this ritual, which lasted several days, tribe members would renew their spiritual beliefs.

At the start of the Sun Dance, a high pole was erected in the center of a lodge or open area, and several dancers would perform around it. The pole symbolized the tribe's connection with nature and paid respect to all growing things.

Coyote and the Dead

In many Native American myths, the coyote is a cunning trickster. This tale comes from the Wishram, an Indian group from the Chinook Mountains of the Pacific Northwest.

When the trickster Coyote's sister died, he grew very sad. Coyote's friend Eagle was also sad because he had lost his wife. Coyote and Eagle decided to travel to the land of the spirits where the dead dwelled. Once there, they would bring back the spirits of their loved ones.

After a long journey, they came to a large body of water where they waited until dark. Coyote began to sing, and soon four spirit men appeared and ferried them across the water to the land of the dead.

There they entered a great tule-mat lodge where the spirits of the dead were dancing and singing under the light of the moon. The spirits were beautifully dressed and their bodies and faces painted. The master of the lodge was Frog, who stood next to the moon inside the lodge.

Early in the morning, the spirits left the lodge for their day of sleep. Coyote seized the moment and killed Frog, putting on his skin. That night the spirits returned to dance and sing. Coyote, in Frog's skin, waited until the celebrations were in full swing and then swallowed the moon.

Free Spirits

In the darkness, Eagle caught the spirits and put them into Coyote's basket. The cunning pair shut the lid tightly, then started back to the land of the living. Coyote carried the basket and Eagle flew overhead, guiding their way. From inside the basket they could hear noises. The spirits were asking to be let out.

Finally the basket got too heavy for Coyote. "Let's let them out," he said, thinking the spirits were so far from the land of the dead that they could not return. So he put down the basket and opened the lid. The spirits immediately flew back to the land of the dead.

At first Eagle was angry with Coyote. Then he said, "It is now fall. The leaves are falling just like the animals die. Let's wait till the spring when everything is new and try to catch them again."

18

Coyote disagreed with Eagle. He thought that the spirits should stay in the land of the dead forever.

Coyote then made a law that a living thing that died could not come to life again. If he had not opened the basket and let the spirits out, then the dead would come to life again every spring, just as grass, flowers, and trees do.

Mount Rainier in Washington State is the home of eagles. These great birds of prey inspired part of this legend.

Tricksters and Shamans

The mysteries of life were celebrated by all Native Americans and specifically by each community's shaman. The shaman was the link between the natural world and the spirit world.

Each Native American tribe had its own animal trickster, which was often a complex and unpredictable character with the traits of its species greatly exaggerated. Coyote was the chief trickster for the Wishram and other tribes. He was cunning, like a real coyote, deceitful, greedy, and ungrateful, but he could also help the Wishram people.

Alongside tricksters were the transformers, who were usually guardian spirits of people. Many tribes thought that the tricksters and transformers were responsible for creating humans.

Linking the Native Americans with the spirit world were the shamans. The shaman was both a medicine man (a healer) and a religious leader. He or she was considered to be in close contact with the spirit world of the ancestors and with the spirits of the natural world, such as the spirits of the corn (maize), the sun, and thunder.

Shamans did their advanced training in inhospitable environments such as this, the Chief Mountain glacier in Montana.

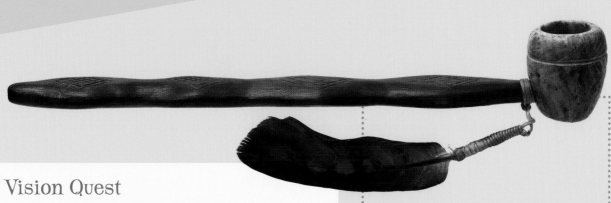

The Vision Quest

Plains tribes, especially the Cheyenne and the Sioux, believed that the spirits could be contacted through a ritual known as the vision quest. It was the shaman's responsibility to help young tribe members perform this rite.

A vision quest could occur several times during a person's lifetime, but traditionally it was felt important for teenage boys—and some girls—to perform the ritual.

Vision quests varied, but typically they began with the youth gathering several items, ranging from grass and herbs to feathers and animal skins, which would then be blessed and specially prepared by the shaman. Next the shaman and the youth smoked tobacco together as an offering to the spirits.

Then the youth would cleanse his or her body, inside and out, by sweating in a sweat lodge, much like a sauna, and drinking an herbal brew that caused vomiting. Finally, the youth journeyed far from camp to fast for several days, during which a spirit guide would appear and teach him or her how to live.

The peace pipe was an important part of the shaman's equipment (see page 42).

This ancient rock painting in the Southwest United States shows a humanlike figure with a headdress and earrings.

The Father of Corn

No other crop was as important to Native Americans as corn, which is durable and easy to grow. This Ojibwa myth provides a divine explanation for the crop's origin.

A long time ago, a poor family lived in the cold land of the Great Lakes. The father was a good man who was grateful to the Great Spirit for everything nature provided, but he was also a bad hunter, and his family often went hungry.

The eldest son, Wunzh, had inherited his father's gentle nature. When he was old enough for the ritual to find the spirit that would guide him through life, he went off to a secluded hut where he had to fast for seven days. He spent the first couple of days admiring the beauty of nature, wondering why some plants were good to eat when others were poisonous.

On the third day, as he lay on his bed, weak from fasting, he saw a young man float down from the sky. The stranger was dressed in a beautiful costume of green and yellow with a plume of waving feathers on his head. The stranger told Wunzh that the Great Spirit had sent him to show Wunzh how to help his tribe survive without hunting and fishing.

The stranger commanded Wunzh to get out of bed and wrestle with him. Although Wunzh felt weak, he wanted to show the stranger that he was brave. He fought until he could fight no more. The stranger said he would return the next day to continue the challenge. After the second time this happened the stranger said he would return once more for a final test.

Strangely, as Wunzh's body had grown weaker each day, his mind had grown stronger. On the seventh day he fought the stranger again, but this time Wunzh won. The stranger took off his beautiful clothes and ordered Wunzh to dig a hole. The stranger climbed into the hole, gave Wunzh a list of instructions, and ordered Wunzh to bury him.

Sound Advice

As the stranger had ordered, Wunzh returned often to water and weed the patch. Through the spring he visited the site, and at the end of summer he took

his father to see it. A large corn plant with bright silken hair and plumes of green leaves nodded in the breeze. Wunzh told his father about the stranger, the challenges, and the instructions on how to grow and harvest corn. He also explained how the corn should be cooked close to the fire until the golden husk turned brown. When the family ate their first meal of corn, they praised the Great Spirit for his gift.

Corn fed the Native American people and inspired some of their most vivid and interesting legends.

Corn and Farming

As the first settlers discovered, Native Americans were expert farmers. Indeed, even in parts of the buffalo-dominated Plains, there were tribes that farmed as well as hunted.

Corn was the most important crop for Native Americans—it could be stored year-round for food, its stalks could be woven into thatch for housing, and its husks could be made into twined blankets. The Ojibwa and other tribes told stories about corn and performed rituals for the planting and harvest seasons.

Corn was first farmed by Mesoamerican tribes thousands of years ago. By the time Christopher Columbus arrived in North America in 1492, the crop was grown by tribes across the whole continent. Planting corn was easy. All it took was forming a small mound of earth, making a deep hole in the mound using a stick, and then dropping four or five kernels of corn into the hole.

By the sixteenth century, many tribes were planting corn alongside other crops such as pumpkins, peppers, gourds, beans, and squashes.

Corn could be grown in all regions except the cold Subarctic and Arctic. In the desert conditions of the Southwest,

Easy to grow and good to eat, pumpkins were an important part of the Native American diet.

the average annual rainfall was as little as 13 inches (33 cm). The Hohokam tribe, which existed from around 300 B.C. until the mid-1400s, built wide, shallow irrigation trenches and dams and valves made of woven mats to control the flow of water onto the fields.

This sixteenth-century picture shows Secota, a Native American town in Virginia.

Farms and Villages

The earliest Native Americans were hunter-gatherers who had no permanent home and were always on the move in search of wild game, berries, or nuts to eat. The development of farming, around 5,500 years ago, changed their lifestyles. They could now settle in one fertile place, build villages, and grow their own food.

Not all tribes settled down. The Plains tribes, for example, lived part of the year in permanent villages and the rest of the time following buffalo herds. They planted their crops in the spring, left the village to hunt buffalo in the summer, and returned to the village in the late fall in time to harvest the crops.

Wisagatcak and the Creation

This Cree myth, which explains how land was created, contains many elements that would have been familiar to Native Americans in the Subarctic, including beaver dams and springs.

One day, Wisagatcak built a dam out of stakes that he placed across a creek. He wanted to trap the Great Beaver when he swam out of his lodge. Wisagatcak waited all day and was getting very bored when finally, as dusk fell, he spotted the Great Beaver swimming toward him and the dam. He took hold of his spear and aimed it at the Great Beaver. Just as he got ready to throw it, a muskrat bit him in the bottom, causing him to miss. Angry and frustrated, Wisagatcak gave up hunting for the night.

The next morning, he decided to break the dam apart, so he took down all the stakes. Water began flowing out, but Wisagatcak could not believe his eyes. The water level was rising instead of falling. He tried desperately to stop the water flowing everywhere, but the Great Beaver had used his magic powers and cast a spell on the water. Soon the whole world was covered with water.

Saving the Animals

Having raced to the top of a nearby mountain, Wisagatcak pulled up hundreds of trees to make a large raft before the water got too deep. Then he helped as many different animals on board as the large raft could carry. These included the muskrat, the raven, and the wolf.

After two relentless weeks, the Great Beaver finally stopped making the water rise. The muskrat volunteered to be the first to leave the raft in search of dry land. He swam for many hours until he grew tired and drowned. Then the raven left the raft. He flew for a whole day looking

The importance of water to Native Americans is illustrated by this story about a great flood.

mouth. As he ran, the moss grew larger and larger until dry land started to form on it. Then the wolf put the land down and all the animals danced around it in circles, singing powerful spells.

The land grew wider and wider in every direction, spreading across the large raft and eventually covering most of the world. Some water remained underneath the earth, however. Whenever water sprang up through holes in the ground, it was said to be because of cracks appearing in Wisagatcak's enormous raft.

for land, but all he could see in every direction was water.

The next day, Wisagatcak decided to use his own magic and asked the wolf to help him. He made the wolf run along the edge of the raft with a ball of moss in his

Water in the Subarctic

Tribes who lived in the Subarctic region relied on lakes and rivers to supply them with fish for food, small game for clothing, and a method of travel.

Water was central to the lives of the Cree and the other Subarctic tribes. They depended on lakes and rivers for sources of food and transportation and thought that all nature contained powerful spirits such as Wisagatcak and the Great Beaver.

This forest lake in Ontario, Canada, is typical Cree territory.

The Subarctic region covers most of Canada's Northwest Territories and the provinces from Manitoba in the west to Newfoundland in the east, and the edge of the Arctic tundra in the north to the Great Lakes in the south. The landscape is made up of thick pine forests interspersed with thousands of rivers and lakes. All the waterways and land freeze over during the winter, which in the extreme north lasts six months.

In the early nineteenth century, when European explorers first made contact with the Cree, the Native Americans' hunting territory stretched from the Ottawa River to the Saskatchewan River, a distance of 1,200 miles (1,920 km). In this vast area, Native Americans hunted moose, caribou, and smaller game such as hare and beaver, and when possible, gathered roots and berries. Farming was difficult because of the harsh winter conditions, but Native Americans adapted their technology to suit the climate.

Five Ojibwa Native Americans paddle a canoe in the Great Lakes region on the US-Canada border.

Fish such as salmon, char, pike, and trout also formed an important part of their diet. During the long winter months, the Cree would camp near frozen lakes and fish through holes in the ice. This gave them food until spring arrived, when they began hunting again.

Adjusting to the Seasons

In summer, the Cree moved their camps in search of animals to hunt. They lived in cone-shaped tents, similar to tepees, that were covered with birchbark. These birchbark tents were lightweight and easy to transport. In winter, the Cree hunted on foot, wearing snowshoes to cross the frozen lakes, rivers, and streams.

Once spring arrived, the land turned boggy as the snow melted. The tribes of the Subarctic and Eastern Woodlands then used canoes to navigate the rivers and lakes. The canoes were made from strips of bark from birch or elm trees.

Raven Steals the Daylight

The Tsimshian tribe, along with others of the Pacific Northwest Coast region, believed that Raven, one of their most important deities, gave daylight to the world.

Long ago, before there was daylight and when the world was covered in darkness, Raven left the heavens and flew across the water for a very long time. As he grew tired he dropped a small stone his father had given him. The stone fell into the sea and turned into a large rock. Then Raven flew east until he reached the mainland. There he scattered salmon and trout roe (eggs) in the rivers so that they would be full of fish. He also dropped seeds onto the land to make plenty of fruit and berries for people.

One night, clouds blocked the little light that the stars gave off. Raven realized how hard it must be for people to look for food in total darkness. To help them, he flew to the house of the Heaven Chief.

He had not been there long when the Heaven Chief's daughter came out with a bucket to fetch water. On seeing her, Raven turned himself into a leaf and dropped into her bucket. Without noticing the leaf, the Heaven Chief's daughter took a drink from the bucket and swallowed it. Immediately she became pregnant. The Heaven Chief and his wife were delighted soon afterward when she gave birth to a strong baby boy.

Light Box

As the baby boy grew, he kept crying and nothing would console him. The Heaven Chief summoned all the wise men of the heavens to ask their advice. One of them said that the baby wanted mã. The mã was the box in a corner of the Heaven Chief's house where light was kept.

The Heaven Chief gave the baby the box, and as soon as he took it, he stopped crying. For the next four days, he played with it happily, but then he started crying again. The Heaven Chief felt sorry for him and asked his daughter what the problem was. She listened to the baby and then told her father that the baby wanted to look at the sky but could not see it because the smoke hole in the ceiling of the house was sealed.

To make the baby happy, the Heaven Chief opened the smoke hole. At once the baby changed back into Raven. Grasping the box containing the daylight, he flew out of the smoke hole and back down to the earth. Raven landed on top of a mountain. Taking the light out of the box, he threw it everywhere, bringing daylight to all the people.

The raven is celebrated in Native American mythology as the creature that brought light to the world.

The Pacific Northwest

The Tsimshian, the Nootka, the Chinook, and the other tribes who lived in the Northwest Coast region had many cultural similarities, such as the potlatch ceremony, and they were expert traders.

The totem pole was an important part of Native American traditions.

The Tsimshian myth (see page 30) of Raven bringing abundance and daylight to people reflected the rich variety of food available to the tribes of the Pacific Northwest Coast. This region, stretching in a narrow band from Yakutat Bay in the Gulf of Alaska to Cape Mendocino in California, offered the greatest quantity and variety of food in North America. The vast array included marine animals, large land mammals such as bear, moose, and elk, and numerous kinds of nuts and berries. For many tribes, however, fish was the main food source, and the fishermen developed a range of methods for catching fish, including trapping, netting, hooking, and spearing.

Totem Poles

Northwest Coast tribes lived in villages and were skilled carpenters best known for carving totem poles. There are several different kinds of totem poles, ranging from memorial ones, which were erected when a house changed owners, to ridicule poles, on which the likeness of an important person who had failed in some way was

A beautiful rainbow arches above a lake in Cree territory in Canada.

carved upside down. They could also be like family crests, where an image on the pole represented an important ancestor.

The Northwest Coast tribes built large houses out of giant cedar trees that they felled and split into planks. In some villages, the whole village might live in the same plank house. The biggest house is thought to have been 650 feet (196 m) long by 60 feet (18 m) wide. In the center was a fire pit used for heating and cooking. The houses were open, but there were moveable screens for greater privacy if anyone wanted it.

POTLATCH CEREMONY

The potlatch was both a religious and a social ceremony held by many Northwest Coast tribes. It was used to celebrate a range of events, including moving into a new house, erecting a totem pole, or a marriage ceremony. The heart of the ceremony was the giving of gifts by the host. This was not done to be generous but to place the receiver of the gift under an obligation to the host.

Following a potlatch, guests were expected to hold a bigger, more lavish potlatch in return. Often this brought either financial ruin or, if they refused to hold their own potlatch, shame.

There was also a spiritual aspect to the potlach ceremony. The food eaten there symbolized links to the spirit world. Eating a lot of salmon, for example, was a show of respect to the divine spirit of fish.

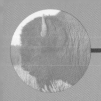

Sedna, Goddess of the Sea

The Inuit depended on fish and sea mammals for survival. They believed that the temperamental goddess Sedna decided whether hunters would have a good catch or not.

Sedna, an Inuit girl, lived alone with her father. She was very beautiful and many men wanted to marry her, but she was vain and refused them all.

One day, a man arrived in the village who was more handsome than any of her other admirers. His kayak was decorated with jewels, and he wore the finest furs and carried a spear of solid ivory. He called to Sedna, "Be my wife and come away with me." He promised her that she would never be hungry or need to work if she married him. Sedna was so impressed that she packed her bags and left with the stranger without telling her father.

For two days they sailed, and during the journey Sedna noticed that her new husband began to change. First his jewels and spear disappeared, then his skin fell away to reveal feathers. His eyes grew beady and feathers covered his face.

When they arrived at his home, his true identity was revealed. He was a bird-spirit. His house was a nest and the meat he brought her was only freshly killed gulls. It was true Sedna did not have to work, but she hated living in the nest and cried when she thought of her father.

Rescue Operation

Meanwhile, her father was lonely and decided to find Sedna. After sailing for many days he found her sitting alone in the nest. The bird-spirit was away hunting. Sedna explained what had happened and together they sailed away.

When the bird-spirit returned to the empty nest, he vowed to reclaim his wife. Flying above the icy sea, it did not take him long to catch up to the boat. Swooping down, he tried to seize Sedna, but her father hit him with an oar. The bird-spirit then flew away. As he went, he created a storm so fierce that Sedna's father was unable to steer the boat.

"The sea is angry because you left your husband," he shouted at Sedna. A mad look came over his face, and he threw his daughter overboard. She clung to the edge of the boat, but her father struck her right hand with his ax, cutting off her fingers. The severed fingers fell into the sea and became seals. Then he hit her left hand and those fingers became whales. Finally, Sedna herself disappeared under the water, where she became the goddess of the sea and ended the storm.

A humpback whale leaps from the North Atlantic Ocean off the coast of Maine.

The Inuit and the Sea

The cold, harsh conditions of the Arctic made life hard for Inuit who lived in the frozen region. Survival often meant taking life-threatening risks, like hunting whales.

The Inuit believed that Sedna, as the goddess of the sea, provided them with most of their food. To keep Sedna happy, the Inuit community held various ceremonies. These rituals varied from time to time and place to place, but they were all based on the belief that angering Sedna might prompt her to stop providing sea mammals for the Inuit to eat.

In the twentieth century, the Inuit still lived in the same way as their ancestors had done 5,000 years ago, when they first crossed the Bering Strait. They depended on the sea for survival and inhabited coastal areas that spread from Siberia, across northern Canada, to Greenland.

In addition to forming the main part of their diet, whales, seals, and walruses also gave the Inuit material for clothing, weapons, fuel, and shelter.

In the long Arctic winter, the Inuit mainly hunted seals. When the sea freezes over,

An Inuit paddles his kayak along the Noatak River in Alaska.

This engraving shows a cluster of igloos forming a traditional Inuit village.

seals make breathing holes in the ice. The hunters would wait by these breathing holes to catch the seals when they came up for air.

In summer, when the ice melts, seals and other sea mammals like walruses are easier to catch because they climb out of the water to sun themselves on land. Inuit hunters crawled up silently behind the mammals and harpooned them.

One of the most dangerous parts of Inuit life was whale hunting. Using umiaks (open wooden boats that usually sat 10 people), the hunters sailed among a small group, or pod, of whales so that the harpooner could get close enough to spear one. Once the whale was injured, the hunters harpooned it several more times until it died. The risk of being capsized while hunting such huge mammals was worth taking because just one large whale could provide tons of meat for a whole community.

Eaters of Raw Meat

Because of the Arctic climate, the Inuit lacked fruits and vegetables, foods that prevent scurvy (a disease caused by the lack of vitamin C). They obtained this vitamin by eating fresh raw meat.

The Girl in the Sky

On the Great Plains, the sky dominates the flat landscape. This Arapaho myth shows the Plains tribe's fascination with both the sky and nature.

One day the young Sapana was gathering firewood. At the bottom of a giant cottonwood tree she saw a porcupine. She wanted its quills for her embroidery, so she tried to catch it. The animal raced up the tree and Sapana followed it.

The tree seemed to go all the way to the sky. When she got to the top, Sapana saw what looked like a shining wall above her. It was the sky. Suddenly she found herself in the middle of a floating camp in the clouds. The porcupine had turned into an ugly old man.

The old man took Sapana to his family's tepee. Once inside he put her to work, scraping buffalo hides and making robes.

Every morning the old man went hunting, leaving Sapana to dig wild turnips. He warned her not to dig too deep, but one day she pulled up a very large turnip that left a hole in the cloud. Carefully replacing the turnip over the hole, Sapana thought up a way to escape.

She began by secretly collecting strips of sinew left over from buffalo hides. She tied them together to make a long rope. Then, while the old man was out hunting, she laid her digging stick across the hole. She tied one end of the rope to the stick and the other around her waist and lowered herself through the hole.

Help from the Birds

Although the rope was long, the floating camp was much higher than Sapana had realized. When she reached the end of the rope she was still far from the ground. She swung in the air, not sure what to do. Then the rope began to shake violently. The old man was pulling at the rope and throwing stones down on her.

Close by, a buzzard circled. Sapana asked him for help. She climbed onto the buzzard's back, and the bird started to descend, but Sapana was too heavy for him. The buzzard called to a hawk, who took Sapana on his back. Soon the hawk

too grew tired, and Sapana got back onto the buzzard. Finally the buzzard dropped her at her village, and before she could thank the birds, they both flew away.

When Sapana's parents saw her, they were very happy. She told everyone about her adventure and the kindness of the buzzard and the hawk. From then on, as a show of thanks to the birds, her tribe always left one animal for the buzzard and the hawk to eat after every successful hunt.

On the Great Plains, the sky dominates the horizon and appears more important than the largely flat and featureless land.

Great Plains, Vast Sky

With its vast, empty spaces and endless horizons, the Great Plains is a landscape dominated by the sky. The mythology and art of the Plains peoples reflects this inescapable fact.

On the Great Plains—an area between the Rocky Mountains and the Mississippi River that stretches from Texas to Alberta, Canada—the land is flat and the horizon can appear miles away. For the Native Americans who roamed this vast region—including the Arapaho, the Assiniboine, the Blackfoot, the Cheyenne, the Comanche, the Crow, the Kiowa, and the Sioux—everything was dominated by the sky. The importance of the sky is reflected in their stories, in the spirits they worshipped, and in the way they lived.

Weather Worship

Many tribes believed that their most important heavenly spirit, the Sky Father, was in everything and everywhere, protecting all the people. Along with the other sky spirits, the Sky Father guided animals along their migration routes and decided when the rivers would flow or dry up.

The Plains tribespeople believed that severe weather, such as lightning, thunderstorms, and hail, were signs of displeasure from the sky spirits. To

This is a typical tepee of South Dakota, where the Arapaho and the Cheyenne lived.

This Native American has a travois pulling device attached to his horse.

Tornadoes were a constant reminder to Native Americans of the power of nature.

keep all the spirits happy, the people performed various ceremonies, including the Sun Dance (see pages 16–17).

Stargazers

The night sky also played an important role in the mythology and lives of Plains tribes. For example, the seminomadic Pawnee—who traveled part of the year in search of buffalo, but kept permanent villages where crops were grown—arranged their lodges in the shape of the constellations. Tepees, shields, and the clothing of all Plains tribes were decorated with stars and the moon.

In myth, the morning star (Venus) was a warrior who cleared the sky before the sun returned from the underworld at the start of each new day. Tepees in most tribal camps on the Great Plains were laid out so that the entrance flaps opened east toward the morning sun.

All four main points of the compass—north, south, east, and west—held great fascination for Plains tribes. East was associated with birth, because it was in that part of the sky that the sun rose. North—which brought cold winds and snow—was associated with old age and death.

The Coming of the Buffalo

No other animal is more closely associated with Native Americans than the buffalo. This Dakota myth illustrates the divine importance the tribe placed on the animal.

One day, two young men were hunting for buffalo on the Great Plains when they saw a lone figure coming toward them from the west. The figure was moving as fast as a buffalo but it did not look like one.

When the figure got close, the men saw that it was a beautiful woman dressed in a buckskin dress with leggings and moccasins. The left side of the woman's hair was tied with coarse buffalo hair and in her right hand she carried a fan of flat sage. She told the two men that she had been sent by the buffalo tribe and that they must go home and prepare a special tepee for her. Once they had finished it, she would visit them, bringing an important gift for their whole tribe.

As the beautiful woman was giving her instructions, one of the men had impure thoughts about her. The woman stared into the man's eyes, and immediately a cloud came down and covered him in mist. When the mist cleared, only the man's skeleton was left. The woman told the other man, frozen with fear, to return to his tribe without looking back.

Natural Rewards

The hunter ran back to camp and told his elders about the beautiful woman. They followed her instructions exactly. Promptly at sunrise the morning after the tepee was finished, the woman entered the camp, this time carrying a large pipe in both hands.

The chiefs greeted her warmly, thanked her for her visit, and invited her into the special tepee. There they offered her a share of all they had, which, because they had killed no buffalo, was only water. The maiden sipped the water, then spoke

Now quite rare, buffalo would once have darkened this plain in vast herds.

to the chiefs. She told them that Wakan'tanka, the chief of the buffalo tribe, looked kindly on them because of their goodness and honesty.

The pipe she had brought was a gift from Wakan'tanka and was to be used as a means of making peace with other nations. She praised the women of the tribe for working hard to keep the families together, and she talked to the children.

Then she turned to the men of the tribe and told them the pipe would help them, but only if they followed her rules. They must always obey the weather and the elements, otherwise nature would take revenge on the tribe. Whenever they needed buffalo, they must smoke the pipe before a hunt. Then they would find plenty to kill.

She lit the pipe and pointed it to the sky in a show of respect to Wakan'tanka, then she pointed it to the ground, where the corn grew. The woman then took a puff from the pipe, passed it to the chiefs, and left the tepee. As she did so, she turned into a white buffalo calf and disappeared.

Living with the Buffalo

In the summer, when buffalo herds stormed across the Great Plains in the thousands, many tribes followed, hunting for the food, clothing, and other things the animal provided.

According to the Dakota Sioux myth (see page 42), the beautiful woman who turned into a white buffalo promised the tribe that if they followed certain rules they would always have enough buffalo to eat. This myth reflected how important buffalo were to the tribe's culture. In fact, buffalo were key to the survival of all Plains tribes, not just as food but also for clothing, weapons, and shelter.

This wild buffalo is one of the protected animals in Yellowstone, a national park in Wyoming, Montana, and Idaho.

Later Hunting Methods

For thousands of years, buffalo were hunted on foot. This was dangerous, because buffalo are fast, strong, and heavy. Weighing as much as 2,000 pounds (1,000 kg), a buffalo could easily trample a person to death.

While hunters in mountainous areas of the West could trick the shortsighted creatures into stampeding over a cliff, there were few natural features on the Plains, and the buffalo could easily run away. Hunting became easier, however, with the arrival of the horse in the seventeenth century.

Summer was the season for buffalo hunting. Every year, the Plains tribes worried about whether they would catch enough buffalo to last them until the next summer. They held rituals to encourage the return of the herds. During the hunt, Sioux leaders carried two good-luck charms—a feathered staff and a buffalo pipe, like the one given by the buffalo woman in the myth.

This painting shows Plains Indians trying to shoot a running buffalo.

USING THE BUFFALO

A dead buffalo offered far more than just cooked and dried meat to the Plains tribes. Warm robes, tepees, and bedding could be made from buffalo hide. Bones could be turned into hand tools, and buffalo hoofs could be boiled down to make a kind of glue. Shields were shaped from the thick skin of a buffalo's neck, and a buffalo's stomach was made into a leak-proof bag for carrying water. The tail could be made into a fly whisk, and the sinews dried and stretched to form strong ropes and cords. Even buffalo dung was useful as a hot, slow-burning fuel.

Glossary

Algonquian The most common Native American language, it originated some 10,000 years ago in the Eastern Woodlands region and spread to the northern Great Plains.

Athapascan Native American language group of western North America. Speakers include some tribes in Canada and the Apache and the Navajo in the Southwest.

Caddoan Native American language that originated in the Southeast but is spoken by tribes who formerly lived west of the Mississippi River, such as the Caddo, the Pawnee, and the Wichita.

Coyote In Wishram mythology, an animal spirit who, with the help of Eagle, killed Frog and tried to steal the spirits of those who had died.

Eastern Woodlands Region that extends from the northern evergreen forests and the Great Lakes and Atlantic areas of Canada and the United States south to the Ohio Valley and west to the Mississippi River. Tribes of the region generally included those who spoke Algonquian, Siouan, or Iroquoian.

Frog In Wishram mythology, he was the master of the lodge where the spirits of the dead dwelled.

Great Beaver In Cree mythology, an animal spirit who caused the old world to flood.

Great Chief In the Iroquoian myth "The Dueling Brothers," he was a mighty sky spirit who banished his wife from their cloud home when he discovered she was pregnant.

Great Chief's wife In the Iroquoian myth "The Dueling Brothers," she was the grandmother of Tsentsa and Taweskare.

Great Plains Vast flat region east of the Rockies that stretches from Texas to Alberta, Canada. It was where the buffalo roamed.

Great Spirit The force behind or present throughout creation; believed in by most tribes, although referred to by different names.

Great Turtle In the Iroquoian myth "The Dueling Brothers," he was leader of the animals on Earth.

Heaven Chief In Tsimshian myth, the keeper of daylight whose daughter is tricked into giving birth to Raven.

Iroquoian One of the two major Native American languages in the Eastern Woodlands region. Speakers include the Cherokee.

Iroquois Confederacy League of Eastern Woodlands tribes made up of the Mohawk, the Oneida, the Onondaga, the Cayuga, the Seneca, and the Tuscarora.

mã Tsimshian mythological box in which daylight was kept. It was stolen from the Heaven Chief by Raven and given to humans.

Mockingbird Hopi spirit who assigned the "ancient people" to different tribes and languages as they escaped from the underworld.

Muskogean The dominant Native American language of the Southeast, spoken by the Chickasaw, the Choctaw, the Creek, and the Seminole peoples.

Northwest Coast Densely forested and mountainous region that stretches thinly southward from the Gulf of Alaska to northern California, and includes tribes such as the Chinook, the Coast Salish, the Haida, the Kwakiutl, the Nootka, the Tlingit, and the Tsimshian.

Old Man Coyote In Crow mythology, he created humans and gave them fire and weapons to use when hunting.

potlatch Ceremony practiced by many Northwest Coast tribes that involved a host throwing a large feast and giving gifts to the guests.

Raven In Tsimshian mythology, a hero spirit who steals daylight from the Heaven Chief for humans.

Sapana In Arapaho mythology, she escaped the cloud home of an ugly old spirit and was rescued by a buzzard and a hawk.

Sedna Inuit goddess of the sea.

Sequoya Born around 1760 and died in 1843, he was the creator of the Cherokee alphabet.

shamans Important members of a tribe who led rituals and were able to call on the spirit world to, among other things, heal the sick.

Siouan A Native American language spoken by the Assiniboine, the Crow, the Iowa, the Osage, and the Dakota, Nakota, and Lakota Sioux, among others. The area that the Siouan languages formerly covered ranged from the Great Lakes to Texas.

Southeast A vast region, extending from the Mississippi River to Florida and from the Gulf of Mexico to Virginia, that included tribes such as the Cherokee, the Chickasaw, the Choctaw, the Creek, and the Seminole.

Southwest A region that covers roughly southern Utah and Colorado, Arizona, New Mexico, west Texas, and northern Mexico, and included Native American peoples such as the Apache, the Hopi, the Navajo, and the Pueblo.

Spider Woman Hopi spirit who, with Mockingbird, helped the "ancient people" escape from the underworld when it was flooding.

Sun Dance Ceremonial dance performed annually by several Plains tribes in order to celebrate and renew their spiritual beliefs.

transformers Mythological characters who were usually guardians of people.

tricksters Complicated mythological characters who could be both troublemakers and heroes.

Tsentsa The mythological father of the Iroquois and the grandson of Great Chief's wife. His younger brother was the angry Taweskare, who made the snakes poisonous.

umiaks Wooden open boats used by Inuit fishermen.

vision quest Grueling ritual, usually performed by young people, intended to introduce a lifelong guide from the spirit world.

Wakan'tanka In Sioux mythology, the spirit chief of the buffalo.

White People A mythological group of ancient Hopi who were the first to see the sun.

Wisagatcak In Cree mythology, he created the current world from atop a giant raft after the old world was flooded by the Great Beaver.

Wunzh In Ojibwa mythology, a young tribesman who was given divine instructions on how to cultivate corn.

Further Information

BOOKS

Bial, Raymond. *Lifeways: The Apache.* Tarrytown, NY: Benchmark Books, 2000.

Clare, John D. *American Indian Life.* Hauppauge, NY: Barrons Juveniles, 2000.

Gibbon, Guy E. *The Sioux: The Dakota and Lakota Nations.* Malden, MA: Blackwell Publishers, 2003.

Hook, Jason, and Richard Hook. *People Who Make History: Native Americans.* Austin, TX: Raintree/Steck Vaughn, 2001.

Murdoch, David. *Eyewitness: North American Indian.* New York, NY: Dorling Kindersley, 2005.

Wishart, David J., ed. *Encyclopedia of the Great Plains Indians.* Lincoln, NE: University of Nebraska Press, 2007.

Yoe, Charlotte, and David Yoe. *The Wigwam and the Longhouse.* Boston, MA: Houghton Mifflin, 2000.

VIDEOS

Biography: Native American Legends. A&E Home Video, 2008.

Native Americans: The Nations of the Northeast. Turner Home Entertainment, 1994.

Native Americans: The People of the Great Plains, Part 1. Turner Home Entertainment, 1994.

Native Americans: Tribes of the Southeast. Turner Home Entertainment, 1994.

WEB SITES

Encyclopedia Mythica: An Encyclopedia on Mythology, Folklore, and Legend
http://www.pantheon.org/areas/mythology/americas/native_american

Mythology of North American Indians
http://www.windows.ucar.edu/tour/link=/mythology/northamerican_culture.html

Index